I Made It Myself!

Papier Mâché Fun

Irène Lassus
Marie-Anne Voituriez

GARETH STEVENS
GS PUBLISHING

A Member of the WRC Media Family of Companies

The author and publishers thank Pierre for the photographs.

Please visit our web site at: www.garethstevens.com
For a free color catalog describing Gareth Stevens Publishing's
list of high-quality books and multimedia programs, call
1-800-542-2595 (USA) or 1-800-387-3178 (Canada).
Gareth Stevens Publishing's fax: (414) 332-3567.

Library of Congress Cataloging-in-Publication Data

Lassus, Irène, 1949-
    [Papier mâché. English]
    Papier mâché fun / Irène Lassus and Marie-Anne Voituriez.
       p. cm. — (I made it myself!)
    ISBN 0-8368-5966-9 (lib. bdg.)
    1. Papier-mâché—Juvenile literature. I. Voituriez, Marie-Anne, 1953- .
II. Title. III. Series.
TT871.L37   2005
745.54'2—dc22   2005046500

This edition first published in 2006 by
Gareth Stevens Publishing
A Member of the WRC Media Family of Companies
330 West Olive Street, Suite 100
Milwaukee, Wisconsin 53212 USA

This U.S. edition copyright © 2006 by Gareth Stevens, Inc.
Original edition first published by Larousse-Bordas, Paris,
France, under the title *Tout en papier: Papier Mâché*,
copyright © Dessain et Tolra / Larousse, Paris 2004.

Photography: Cactus Studio
Translation: Muriel Castille
English text: Dorothy L. Gibbs
Gareth Stevens series editor: Dorothy L. Gibbs
Gareth Stevens art direction and cover design: Tammy West
Gareth Stevens graphic design: Jenni Gaylord

Printed in the United States of America

1 2 3 4 5 6 7 8 9 09 08 07 06 05

CONTENTS

Making Papier-Mâché

The name "papier-mâché" comes from a French word that means "chew" or "tear apart." Making papier-mâché, however, does not mean you will have to chew paper. You will simply have to tear paper of various kinds into strips or small pieces. Then all you have to do is stick the torn paper onto a shape of some kind with glue. So, don't let the unusual name worry you. Papier-mâché is easy — and a lot fun!

Materials:

- powdered wallpaper paste
- water
- glass jar (to mix the glue in)
- wooden stick (to stir the glue)
- newspapers, magazines, kraft*
  paper, and other types of paper

Prepare wallpaper glue for your papier-mâché by mixing powdered wallpaper paste with water in a glass jar (following the directions on the box of wallpaper paste). Tear up enough strips or small pieces of newspaper, magazine pages, or any other kind of paper to entirely cover the shape you will be using. The shape can be made out of newspaper or aluminum foil, or it can be an object, such as a plate, a glass, a box, or a balloon.

Using your fingertips, coat the strips or pieces of paper with glue. Stick the glue-coated strips or pieces of paper onto your shape until the shape is completely covered with paper. As you are gluing the paper onto the shape, overlap the pieces and smooth them out to get rid of excess glue and any air bubbles.

Let the paper dry very well before painting or varnishing your shape or adding any other finishing touches.

*Kraft paper is strong, heavy paper,
 like the kind used for paper bags.

Hen and Chick

A big hen and a little chick sharing a nest of shredded paper make a delightful kitchen decoration. And here's another good idea! At Eastertime, put some chocolate eggs into the nest, then hide the hen and chick in your house or garden. Some lucky Easter egg hunter will find a nice surprise!

Materials:
- newspaper
- masking tape
- scissors
- thin red cardboard
- white glue and wallpaper glue
- white and green kraft paper
  (for the hen and the nest)
- bright yellow paper (for the chick)
- blue marker or paint
- empty round cheese box

Scrunch newspaper to make two balls, one big ball (the hen's body) and one small ball (the hen's head). Wrap masking tape around each ball to make sure it holds its shape. Tape the two balls together.

(For the chick, make only one small newspaper ball. Then follow the same instructions given for the hen in steps 2 and 3.)

Cut a comb and a beak out of red cardboard and glue them in place on the hen's head. Cover the hen with small pieces of white kraft paper. Coat each scrap of paper with wallpaper glue before sticking it onto the hen.

To make the tail and the wings, cut long strips of white paper, curl them with the side of closed scissors blades, then glue the curled paper in place. Draw eyes on the hen's head with blue marker or paint. To make the nest, cover an empty round cheese box with glue-coated pieces of green kraft paper. If you like, you can fill the nest with shreds of white paper, which are sold at arts and crafts stores.

Creeping Crocodile

A paper towel roll, some corrugated cardboard, and a little paint can make a really cute crocodile. And this crocodile won't bite! Remember that the crocodile is made of paper, so don't put it in water.

Materials:
- newspaper
- masking tape
- empty roll from paper towels
- white glue and wallpaper glue
- scissors
- white corrugated cardboard
- green and orange paints
- white paper
- black marker

Make shapes for the different parts of the crocodile out of scrunched newspaper: 4 balls for the legs, 2 smaller balls for eyeballs, and 2 long rolls for the head and the tail. Wrap masking tape around all the shapes to hold them together and to make them stronger.

Stick the head and the tail shapes inside each end of an empty paper towel roll. Tape the shapes securely to the roll and tape the legs and the eyeballs in place on the body. Cover the entire crocodile with small pieces of torn newspaper. Be sure that you coat each scrap of newspaper with wallpaper glue.

Cut strips of corrugated cardboard and glue them onto the back and sides of the crocodile's body. Paint the crocodile and let it dry. Cut two round circles out of white paper and glue them onto the eyeballs. Use black marker to draw pupils on the white circles. Cut a thin strip of white corrugated cardboard and glue it to the front and side edges of the head to make teeth.

Cash Stash

If you don't have a piggy bank to keep your coins in, you might want to make this colorful cash box. Decorate the box with pictures of toys you would like to buy. Seeing the pictures on the box will be a daily reminder to keep saving your money!

Materials:
- small cardboard box
- newspaper
- wallpaper glue
- yellow paint
- scissors
- toy catalog
- varnish

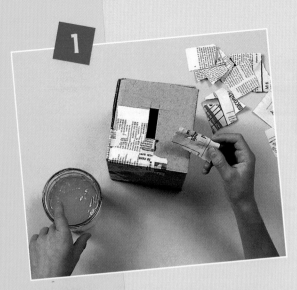

1

Ask an adult to cut a wide slit in the top of a small cardboard box. Cover the entire box with overlapping pieces of torn newspaper. Coat each scrap of paper with wallpaper glue before sticking it onto the box. Let the glued paper dry completely.

2

Paint the box yellow and let the paint dry thoroughly.

3

Cut pictures of toys you like out of a catalog and glue them all over the outside of the painted box. After everything is very dry, coat the whole box with varnish to protect it. When you need to take money out of your box, just turn it upside down and shake out the coins.

Pretty Pots

Look at what you can do with empty jam and jelly jars! Three easy steps is all it takes to turn them into flower pots or vases, and recycling the glass jars is good for the environment. Add some pretty flowers or a small plant to make a great Mother's Day or birthday gift for Mom or Grandma.

Materials:
- clean, empty glass jar
- newspaper
- wallpaper glue
- acrylic paints
- pencil
- varnish

Cover the outside of a clean, empty glass jar with small pieces of torn newspaper. Coat each scrap of paper with wallpaper glue before sticking it onto the jar and be sure to overlap the pieces and smooth them out to get rid of any air bubbles. Let the glue-coated paper dry thoroughly.

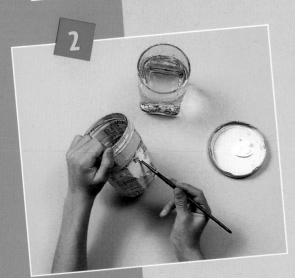

Brush a coat of white paint all over the papier-mâché surface and let the paint dry completely.

Draw designs on the white paint in pencil, then paint the designs, using a variety of bright colors. When the paint is dry, add a coat of varnish to protect your painted designs. The varnish will give your pot a shiny, waterproof surface.

Paper Pearls

A necklace of lightweight paper pearls can be as long as you like with beads as big as you like. It's easy to make, and you can pick colors that match your clothes. Or would you rather make yourself a star? That's easy, too! Just put a picture of yourself in the center of a cardboard star and decorate the edges of the star with tiny paper pearls. Trace the star pattern on page 24 to get started.

Materials:
- tissue paper in many colors
- thin, wooden sticks (or skewers)
- wallpaper glue
- varnish
- strong, thin cord
  or elastic thread

Tear sheets of tissue paper, in all your favorite colors, into narrow strips. Tissue paper is very thin so be sure you tear it carefully. As you tear the paper, remember that the wider the strip of tissue, the bigger the pearl will be.

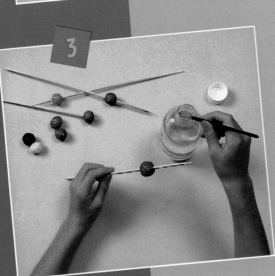

To make each pearl, wrap tissue paper strips around a thin, wooden stick. (A wooden kitchen skewer works very well for this project). The strips must overlap each other. As you wrap, dab small amounts of wallpaper glue on the paper strips to hold them together. The size of the pearl depends on how many paper strips you overlap. Let each pearl dry thoroughly.

Varnish each pearl to give it a shiny protective coating. When the varnish on all the pearls is completely dry, slide them off the wooden sticks and string them onto a piece of strong, thin cord or elastic thread. The cord or thread can be any length you want, but be sure it is long enough to fit over your head after you string the pearls and tie the ends of the cord or thread together.

Fire Truck

Papier-mâché to the rescue! A cardboard box, a couple of corks, and some clay are the main materials you will need to make this clever toy fire truck. To complete your fire truck, cut long and short strips of white cardboard and glue them together to make a ladder.

Materials:
- scissors
- red paper
- wallpaper glue
- small cardboard box
- white kraft paper
- acrylic or poster paints
- air-dry modeling clay
- 2 corks
- 2 long wooden skewers
- 1 yard (1 meter) of clear plastic tubing

1 Cut red paper into rectangles and squares and glue them all over the outside of a small cardboard box. Be sure to coat each scrap of paper with wallpaper glue and overlap the pieces as you stick them onto the box. Cut out eight squares of white kraft paper for side windows and a rectangle for a front windshield and glue them onto the box. Paint the inside of the box red.

2 To make wheels for your truck, flatten four balls of clay into round circles. The circles should be about 3 inches (8 centimeters) across. Leave the clay circles out in the air to dry, then ask an adult to drill a little hole through the middle of each circle. Also ask an adult to cut thin slices of cork off of round bottle corks. You will need eight slices of cork.

3 Paint the cork circles and the outsides of the wheels black. Paint the centers of the wheels red. Ask an adult to drill 4 small holes in the bottom of the box (2 holes on each long side) for the wheels, then cut a hole in the front of the box. Push a wooden skewer through each set of side holes. At each end of the skewers, put a cork slice, then a wheel, then another cork slice. Stick clear plastic tubing into the hole on the front of the box for the fire hose.

Colorful Candy Dishes

Flowers and candy have always been a good combination, so a colorful, flower-shaped dish is the perfect place to keep your candy. Start with a paper plate. The rest is up to you and your imagination.

Materials:
- pencil
- paper plate
- scissors
- newspaper
- wallpaper glue
- white tissue paper
- different colored inks

Draw the shapes of flower petals around the border of a paper plate, then cut along the lines to turn the paper plate into a flower.

Cover the plate with pieces of torn newspaper. Coat each piece with wallpaper glue and overlap the pieces as you stick them onto the plate. On top of the newspaper, stick on a layer of white tissue paper pieces. Let all of the glue-coated paper dry thoroughly.

Now all you have to do is decorate the plate. Brush on colorful inks to make the plate any kind of flower you like. When the ink has dried, you can put candy in the dish, but you just might decide that your flower is too pretty to cover up.

Very Hairy Hedgehog

Some afternoon, if you want to have fun, make some tiny rolls of paper. You can string the rolls onto cord or elastic thread to make a fancy necklace — or you can use them to put hair on a hedgehog!

Materials:
- aluminum foil
- blue and orange kraft paper
- wallpaper glue
- scissors
- long wooden skewers
- red tissue paper

Make a big ball of aluminum foil. Shape the ball like a potato and flatten one side. Then, at one end, shape a stubby point. Cover the foil shape with torn pieces of blue kraft paper. Coat each piece of paper with wallpaper glue before sticking it onto the foil and overlap the pieces of paper as you stick them on. This shape will be the hedgehog's body.

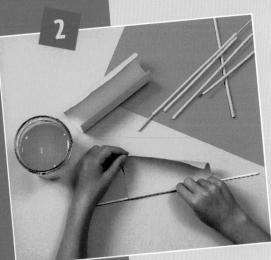

Cut some orange kraft paper into rectangles. Roll up a wooden skewer inside each rectangle and glue the end of the paper to keep it tightly wrapped around the skewer. When you roll the paper around the skewers, leave a little of each skewer uncovered at one end.

Push the unwrapped end of each skewer into the hedgehog's body, covering the back of the hedgehog with spiky hairs. Finish the hedgehog by gluing a ball of red tissue paper onto the stubby point of the body for a nose. (To make the red ball, see the instructions for Paper Pearls on pages 14 and 15.)

Gigantic Candy

Balloons can make any time party time. Here's a fantastic new way to use a balloon to make a party decoration. Blow up the balloon and turn it into a big, pink, piece of candy that you can hang from the ceiling!

Materials:
- round balloon
- wallpaper glue
- newspaper
- scissors
- pink kraft paper
- clear tape
- ribbon
- adhesive-backed paper in several bright colors

Blow up a round balloon and cover it with two layers of glue-coated newspaper. While the newspaper is drying, cut two rectangles out of pink kraft paper and fold each one like an accordion. Wrap clear tape around one end of each folded rectangle to hold it closed, making the rectangle look like a fan. The fans are the ends of the candy wrapper.

When the newspaper on the balloon is completely dry, attach a long piece of ribbon to the middle of the balloon with clear tape. Cover the entire balloon with torn pieces of pink kraft paper. Coat each piece of paper with wallpaper glue and overlap the pieces as you stick them onto the newspaper. Let the pink layer of paper dry.

When the pink paper is completely dry, ask an adult to cut a slit into each side of the covered balloon. The balloon will pop when the slits are cut, but the paper will keep its round shape. Stick a pink fan into each slit to finish the candy wrapper. Cut shapes of all kinds out of colorful, adhesive-backed paper and stick them all over the pink paper to decorate your gigantic piece of candy.

star
(page 14)